the Art of Creating

Ideas for Making Albums, Notebooks, Notes and Binders

WHITE STAR PUBLISHERS

Contents

THE TOOLS	4
ALBUMS AND BINDERS	6
The Watercolor Album	8
The Ballerina's Album	10
An "Engraved" Cover	12
A Star-shaped Album	14
An Eco-friendly Album	18
A Binder for CDs	20
An Album-Game	22
A Moroccan Album	24
The Golden Host's Book	26
The Athlete's Album	28
A Priceless Herbarium	30
The Trompe-l'œil Album	32
The Wedding Album	34

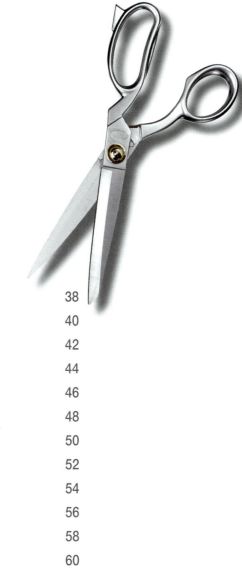

NOTEBOOKS, PADS AND ADDRESS BOOKS	38
A Blue and Gold Notebook	40
The Lighthouse Notebook	42
A Woven Cover	44
The Fall Note Pad	46
Poppies on a Notebook	48
The Secret Diary	50
A Pocket Note Pad	52
Sea-colored Note Pads	54
The Faux Leather Cover	56
A "Precious" Address Book	58
A Rétro Note Pad	60
A Travel Address Book	62

The Tools

Those who don't have memorable photographs to conserve, small objects to carefully store, notes, phone numbers, and addresses to record with precision and keep within arms reach raise your hand. In the following pages, you will find a variety of interesting ideas for making albums, binders, notebooks and address books, where to record memorable moments and useful information. The detailed instructions in this book will give you all the necessary tools for creating anything you need all on your own.

- Alphabet stencil
- Animal stamps
- B hardness pencil
- Black marker
- Bone folder
- Calligraphy pen
- Card stock
- Circle-cutter
- Clear acrylic round label stamp
- Color markers
- Compass
- Compass with adaptor
- Cursive writing stamp
- Cutting mat
- Decorative corner craft punch
- Decorative edge scissors, decker
- Decorative edge scissors, long (8 in. [20 cm])

- Decorative edge scissors, zig zag
- Decorative edge scissors, short (5 1/4 in. [13.5 cm])
- Decoupage scissors
- Eraser
- Fine sandpaper
- Fine-tipped paintbrush
- Flat-tipped paintbrush
- Flower stamp
- Flowering branch stamp
- Glue stick
- Hand-held hole punch (1/8 in. [3 mm] in diameter)
- Hatpin
- Heart stamp
- Hole punch small diameter
- Hole punch (1/4 in. [6 mm] in diameter)

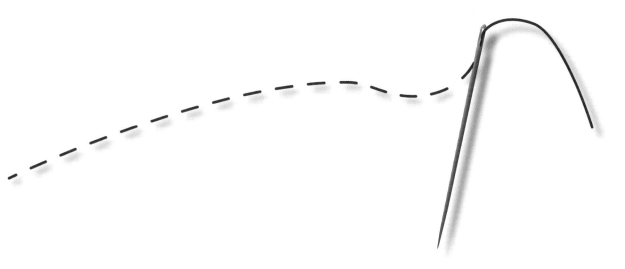

- Hole punch (9/32 in. [7 mm] in diameter)
- Ink pads
- Large needed with rounded tip
- Leaves stamp
- Needle
- Paper clamp
- Paper trimmer
- Pencil
- Piercing tool
- Pink glitter glue pen
- Plexiglas block
- Precision knife
- Removable tape
- Repositionable spray adhesive
- Riveting kit
- Riveting kit with punch (1/4 in. [5 mm] in diameter)
- Rotary cutter
- Round corner craft punch
- Round-tipped paintbrush
- Rubber bands
- Ruler
- Scissors
- Scratchboard tool
- Shoebox
- Sponge
- Star stamp
- Template for cutting concentric circles
- Template for cutting concentric ovals
- Tracing paper
- Clear tape
- Triangle ruler
- Utility knife
- Yellow pencil

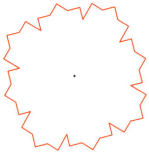

Albums and Binders

The Watercolor Album

Tools
- Pencil
- Ruler
- Precision knife
- Cutting mat

Materials
- 6x4 in. (15x10.5 cm) watercolor album
- A4 white paper
- Light blue A4 natural paper
- Two light blue hair ties
- Universal fast-drying adhesive
- Repositionable spray adhesive

Diff./Time

Easy

1 hour

To conserve your watercolors, construct an album with a natural paper cover supplied with a window.

1 Prepare the Cover

Compose the text on the computer using the desired font, arranging the writing in two lines about 1 1/2 in. (4 cm) apart. Print the text on a piece of white paper. Cut the paper to the same size as the album cover. Glue it to the cover. Trace a 1 3/8x2 1/4 in. (3.5x5.8 cm) opening in the center and cut it out (both in the white paper and the cover).

Cut the Opening in the Covering

Place the album with the cover flat onto the light blue paper. Cut the paper about 3/8 in. (1 cm) from the edges of the cover. Trace the edges of the opening with a pencil. Remove the album. Draw lines about 5/8 in. (15 mm) from those already in place. Using the precision knife, incise this larger opening starting with the corners and cutting one side at a time. Pass the blade over the lines several times to cut without forcing.

IDEA. You can write the text using a calligraphy pen and some blue ink.

2 Glue the Covering

Spray the light blue natural paper covering with spray adhesive. Adhere the paper to the album cover aligning the openings.

3 Cut the Covering

Place the album on the cutting mat with its cover flat and trim excess paper. Close the cover and slide the hair ties onto two opposite sides of the album.

The Ballerina's Album

Tools
- Pencil
- Scissors
- Decorative edge scissors

Materials
- 9x6 1/4 in. (23x16 cm) album with pink cover
- 4x8 1/4 in. (10.5x21 cm) pink card stock
- 5 1/2x23 1/2 in. (14x60 cm) white tissue paper
- A4 white paper
- A4 tracing paper
- 8 in. (20 cm) of 3/8 in. (1 cm) wide pink silk ribbon
- 8 in. (20 cm) of 1/8 in. (3 mm) wide pink silk ribbon
- Universal fast-drying adhesive

Diff./Time

Easy

1 hour

Decorate the cover of a photo album dedicated to the recitals of a budding ballerina with a tutu and ballet shoes.

1 Cut the Components

Copy and trace the ballet shoes (exterior) and the bodice of the tutu onto pink paper. Copy and trace the interior of the shoes onto white paper. Cut out the templates with scissors. Make a color photocopy of the title and cut along the outline with decorative edge scissors leaving a 1/8 in. (3 mm) margin all around.

SUGGESTION. Type the title for the cover on the computer and print it.

2 Make the Tutu

Pleat the strip of white tissue paper creating more or less even 3/8 in. (1 cm) folds. Cut the folded strip into two along height. Glue the two pieces together by applying a line of fast-drying adhesive along one of the final folds. Press together the top of the skirt and glue to the bodice.

Enlarge the shapes by 285% in a photocopier.

3 Decorate the Cover

Make three small 3/4 in. (2 cm) bows from the 1/8 in. (3 mm) wide ribbon and a 4 in. (10 cm) bow from the 3/8 in. (1 cm) wide ribbon. Glue the larger bow to the top of the skirt and one small bow to the right strap. Glue the white shoe templates over the pink. Glue the remaining two small bows to the shoes. Glue the title, the tutu and the shoes to the cover of the album.

Gluing the Components

All the pieces in this project are glued using a fast-drying adhesive. As an alternative, you can use glue drops, double-sided tape or glue tape. Make sure to evenly coat the entire surface of the paper components with glue to ensure they don't peel away during album use.

An "Engraved" Cover

Tools

- Pencil
- Ruler
- Precision knife
- Cutting mat
- Decorative edge scissors
- Riveting kit with punch, 1/4 in. (5 mm) in diameter
- Scratchboard tool

Materials

- Passport photo
- Two 6 1/4x9 in. (16x23 cm) scratchboards
- White sheets for the album's pages (110 g/m2)
- White and black fine point markers
- White chalk
- Two binder rings
- 8 in. (20 cm) of 1/16 in. (2 mm) wide thin black ribbon
- Removable tape
- Repositionable spray adhesive
- Universal fast-drying adhesive

Diff./Time

Medium

2 hours

Collect photos and mementos from an important year in an album with a cover created using the scratchboard technique.

1 Prepare the Templates

On a sheet of 80 g/m2 paper, draw one 4 1/8x2 7/8 in. (10.5x7.2 cm) rectangle and one 4x6 in. (10x15 cm) rectangle. Draw smaller rectangles 1/4 in. (5 mm) from the initial lines. Cut along the outside of the bigger frame and along the inside of both using a precision knife. Cut out the smaller frame using scissors. Using the same method, trace and cut-out parts of other frames of various sizes. From the passport photo, cut away the background around the face leaving a 1 1/2x2 in. (4x5 cm) frame all around. Photocopy the paperclip and the four triangles, and cut them out. Try different compositions, arranging all the components on one of the scratchboards.

2 Transfer the Templates

Apply a thin coat of spray adhesive to the back of the frames, frame sections and triangles. Glue these components to the scratchboard. Secure the cut-out silhouette with small pieces or repositionable tape. Using the scratchboard tool and a ruler, incise the outline of the triangles and the two frames (except where they overlap). Color the back the paper clip with white chalk. Position the component on the scratchboard, trace its outlines with a pencil and remove them. Using the white fine point marker, retrace the white chalk lines.

Enlarge the drawings by 300% in a photocopier.

TRICK. *Use black and white markers to touch up the final drawings.*

3 Incise the Motifs

Detach the frames and the triangles from the board. Fill in the paperclips along the side of one of the frames, the 90° angle of the triangles, the background of the silhouette, the largest frame, one frame fragment.

4 Assemble the Album

Overlay the two scratchboards, back to back. Using the punch and hammer, make holes along the left side, 1/2 in. (1.2 cm) from the edge and at an equal distance from the top and bottom. Using the black marker, color the edges of the boards. Using a precision knife, incise a 1/8 in. (3 mm) long slit centered along height and 5/8 in. (1.5 cm) from the edge opposite the one with the holes in each cover. Cut the ribbon in half and insert the end of each half into the slits. Secure the ribbons to the back of the covers by gluing a circle of white paper on top. Cut 6 1/8x8 7/8 in. (15.5x22.5 cm) rectangles from white paper. Overlay the covers and the white paper rectangles making sure the holes coincide. Insert the rings into the holes and lock them.

Use the Scratchboard Technique

This graphics technique employs a tool with a thin point, which is used to scratch a white board coated with black ink to produce drawings composed of white lines. By altering the pressure applied and the angle of the tool, you can obtain strokes of various thicknesses.

A Star-shaped Album

Tools

- Pencil
- Eraser
- Ruler
- Utility knife
- Cutting mat
- Paper trimmer
- Bone folder
- Flat-tipped paintbrush
- Scissors
- Hole punch (1/4 in. [6 mm] in diameter
- Flowering branch stamp
- Clear acrylic round label stamp
- Plexiglas block
- Rubber bands

Materials

- 2x3 in. (5x8 cm) color photos
- A4 Finnboard, 1/32 in. (1 mm) thick
- Scrapbooking paper with two different patterns
- 20x25 1/2 in. (50x65 cm) red, orange and yellow card stock, (120 g/m2)
- Green paper
- Brown ink pad
- 15 3/4 in. (40 cm) of 3/8 in. (1 cm) wide orange satin ribbon
- Three 3/8 in. (1 cm) wide satin ribbons of various colors and patterns
- Double-sided tape
- Elmer's glue

Diff./Time

Difficult

3 hours

Explanation on 2 spreads

Nothing is more original than an album that transforms into a star to keep memorable vacation photos.

PREPARE THE INSIDE

TRICK. This album is also a decorative object: to keep it open, tie the two ribbons together.

1 Cut the Paper

Using the paper trimmer, cut six 4x10 in. (10x25 cm) red, six 4x8 in. (10x20 cm) orange and six 4x6 in. (10x15 cm) yellow rectangles from the solid card stock. Cut two 4 1/8x5 1/8 in. (10.5x13 cm) rectangles from the finnboard with a utility knife.

2 Fold the Paper

Score the central fold in each card stock rectangle using a bone folder. Fold in half as if making standard greeting cards.

3 Assemble the Cards

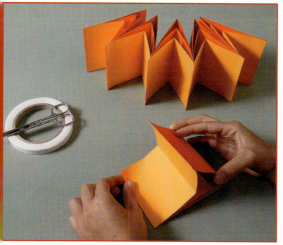

Assemble the yellow, orange and red cards into sets of three using strips of double-sided tape.

Construct the Pages

Attach two strips of double-sided tape to the exterior of each yellow and orange card, along longer edges. Adhere the edges of the yellow cards to the inside edges of the orange cards (perform this step carefully: the edges must align perfectly). In the same way, attach the edges of the orange cards to the inside edges of the red cards. To unite the sets of pages, attach a strip of double-sided tape to the outer left edges of five red cards (attaching double-sided tape to the last red card is not necessary because this page will be glued directly to the cover).

ASSEMBLE THE ALBUM

1 Wrap the Covers

Cut two 5 1/8x6 1/8 in. (13x15.5 cm) rectangles from the patterned scrapbooking paper. Brush Elmer's glue onto the finnboard rectangles. Glue the finnboard rectangles to the center of the patterned scrapbooking paper rectangles. Cut away the paper corners about 1/8 in. (3 mm) from the foam board. Brush the glue onto the paper flaps and fold them around the finnboard edge. Press down well and allow to dry under a weight.

2 Attach the Ribbon

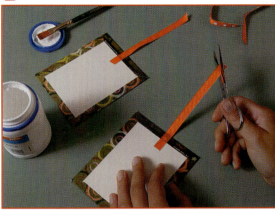

Cut two 6 1/4 in. (16 cm) long strips of orange ribbon. Brush Elmer's glue onto the final 1 1/4 in. (3 cm) of one of the ends of both ribbons. Glue the ribbons to the inside of the covers centering along the shorter edges.

3 Attach the Covers

Spread the glue onto one cover (the uncovered side). Adhere one of the outer red pages. In the same way, apply glue to the other cover and glue on the other outer red page. Close the album and keep it well compressed with rubber bands for at least one hour.

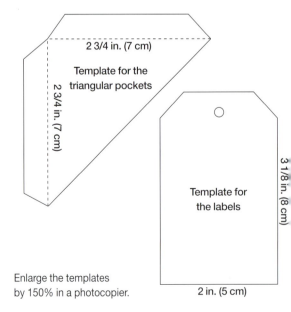

2 3/4 in. (7 cm)
Template for the triangular pockets
2 3/4 in. (7 cm)

Template for the labels
3 1/8 in. (8 cm)
2 in. (5 cm)

Enlarge the templates by 150% in a photocopier.

DECORATE THE ALBUM

4 Glue the Triangular Pockets

On the back of the other sheet of scrapbooking paper, draw six pockets with a pencil using the diagram as a guide. Cut out and score along the folds with a bone folder. Fold the flaps and coat them with Elmer's glue. Glue the pockets to the lower left corners of the pages.

6 Glue the Rectangular Pockets

From the same scrapbooking paper as the triangular pockets, cut strips 3 3/8 in. (8.5 cm) long and 1 1/2 in. (4 cm) wide. Fold 3/16 in. (5 mm) flaps at the short ends. Brush the flaps with glue and adhere the pockets to the lower right of the pages.

8 Decorate the Cover

5 Make the Rectangular Labels

Photocopy the label and cut it out. Position this template onto scraps of red or orange card stock, or onto the green paper, and trace with a pencil. Cut out with a utility knife. Make a hole using the hole punch where indicated. Insert a ribbon into each label and tie it off.

7 Make the Round Labels

Adhere the clear acrylic round label stamp to the Plexiglas block. Ink with the brown ink pad and stamp the design on orange card stock scraps or on the green paper. Allow to dry. Trim close to the stamped circle. Using the hole punch, make a hole close to the edge. Insert a ribbon into each label and knot. Ink the flowering branch stamp and stamp the design on the pages of the album and on the rectangular labels.

IDEA. You can arrange the photos on paper rectangles of a contrasting color and cut them out using decorative edge scissors.

Glue a photo, the title typed on the computer and printed on white paper, and a round label with the place, date and event at which the photo was taken to the cover. Secure the components using double-sided tape or glue.

An Eco-friendly Album

Tools
- Pencil
- Ruler
- Utility knife
- Cutting mat
- Scissors
- Riveting kit
- Hatpin
- Sponge

Materials
- Recycled card stock
- C5 Havana Kraft paper envelopes
- Patterned scrapbooking paper (A and B)
- Orange, brown and pink paper
- Alphabet stickers (three different sheets)
- FOR THE DECORATIONS: strings, buttons, ribbons, pieces of fabric, colored rivets, crown corks, dry leaves and flowers
- Double-sided tape
- Universal fast-drying adhesive
- Spray adhesive

Diff./Time

Medium

2 hours and 30 min.

With different recycled materials (fabric, buttons, bottle caps etc.), you can create an original album stocked with many pockets.

1 Cut the Components

Cut out two 6 1/4x8 3/4 in. (16x22 cm) rectangles from the card stock. Insert the card stock into two Kraft paper envelopes and glue down the flaps. Cut two 6 1/4x12 in. (16x30.5 cm) rectangles from scrapbooking paper A, two 2 3/8x8 3/4 in. (6x22 cm) strips from scrapbooking paper B, and two 6 1/4x8 3/4 in. (16x22 cm) from the solid paper. Cut two 4x6 1/4 in. (10x16 cm) rectangles from the fabric.

Have Fun Reusing Objects!
Cereal boxes, for example, can be used in many of your projects. Use them, as in this case, to make covers for albums or notebooks, or for making stencils. Crown bottle caps will prove an original decorating element: flatten them with a hammer and if you wish, color them using ink pads.

2 Wrap the Cover

The decorations on the two envelops should be mirror images of each other. Spray one envelope (the front) with spray adhesive and adhere one rectangle of scrapbooking paper A, folding a 3 in. (7.5 cm) flap around the edge. Glue the solid paper to the back of the envelope (first lift the flap). Pour a line of fast-drying adhesive along three edges of the strip of scrapbooking paper B and adhere it to the envelope (front) to form a pocket. Glue a rectangle of fabric next to it, folding the excess around the edge. Pierce the center of the flap with the hatpin and insert a string. Secure the flap and the string to the envelope with a strip of double-sided tape. Apply the rivets: one along the lower edge of the pocket and the other along the opposite edge of the envelope. Glue a 1 1/2x6 3/8 in. (4x16.2 cm) strip of solid paper to the back.

3 Make the Pages

From solid paper, cut two rectangles: one 6 3/8x9 5/16 in. (16.2x23.6 cm) and one 6 3/8x8 3/4 in. (16.2x22 cm). Spray the smaller rectangle with spray adhesive and glue it to the back of an envelope. Glue the larger to the front of an envelope, aligning it with the flap and folding the excess around the edge. Trim away excess paper following the outline of the flap. Decorate with strips of patterned scrapbooking paper.

TRICK. *You can make an album with six or seven "pages". If you leave the envelope flaps open, it will be possible to store some photos inside.*

4 Make the Hinge

Make reference marks 3/8 in. (1 cm) from the left edge, and 1 1/2 in. (4 cm) from the top and bottom borders of the covers and the pages. Using the riveting kit, punch holes in correspondance with the marks. Place the pages between the covers and align the holes. Insert strings into the holes and tie them securing the album together.

5 Decorate the Album

Decorate the page flaps with a square of patterned paper or a flattened crown bottle cap. Compose the text on the cover using adhesive letters (use letters from different sheets). Attach photographs, decorations and short phrases to the pages. Decorate the cover with buttons and dry leaves and flowers. Insert two photos into the pocket. Tie ribbons to the rivets.

A Binder for CDs

Tools

- Pencil
- Ruler
- Circle-cutter
- Rotary cutter
- Precision knife
- Cutting mat
- Scissors
- Bone folder
- Riveting kit

Materials

- 12 3/4x19 3/4 in. (32.5x50 cm) black foam board, 3/16 in. (5mm) thick
- 19 3/4x25 1/2 in. (50x65 cm) sheets of fuchsia, turquoise, acid green, brown and silver paper
- A4 acetate with a turquoise pattern
- Permanent black marker
- Stickers of different colors, 3/16 in. (5 mm) in diameter
- Metal binder rings, 1 1/2 in. (4 cm) in diameter
- Rubber cement
- Adhesive tape

Diff./Time

Medium

2 hours

Craft this original CD case with a foam board cover and pages with two-colored pockets.

1 Cut the Components

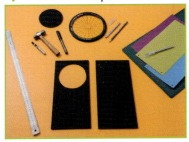

Obtain two 6x12 in. (15x30 cm) rectangles of black foam board. Using the punch and the hammer, make two holes in the rectangles 9/32 in. (7 mm) from the short edges and 1/2 in. (12 mm) from the long edges. Using a pencil, divide one of the rectangles into halves, forming two 6 in. (15 cm) squares. In the left square, cut a 4 3/4 in. (12 cm) circle using the circle-cutter and the rotary cutter. Color the edges with a black marker. From colored paper, cut 6x12 in. (15x30 cm) pages. Cut 3/4x6 in. (2x15 cm) strips of colored paper and glue them to the left edges of the pages. Make holes in the pages as you did for the cover.

2 Decorate the Cover

Cut a 6 in. (15 cm) square of turquoise patterned acetate. Glue it to the back of the cover, in correspondance with the round opening. Cut a 6 in. (15 cm) square from the turquoise paper. Glue it to the foam board rectangle, next to the opening. From the acid green paper, cut one 4 3/4 in. (12 cm) circle and one 6 in. (15 cm) circle using the circle cutter, obtaining a 1 1/4 in. (3 cm) thick ring. Glue the ring in correspondance with the round opening. Cut out a silver ring with a diameter of 4 3/4 in. (12 cm) and glue it to the center of the turquoise square. Attach colorful stickers to the center of the circles.

Enlarge the pocket and closure flap by 500% in a photocopier.

TRICK. *If you don't have a circle-cutter, use a template for drawing concentric circles or a compass with an adaptor into which you can insert a rotary cutter.*

3 Cut Out the Initials

To cut out the C, position the center of the circle-cutter on the edge of the fuchsia paper. Insert the rotary cutter into hole 25 and cut a semi-circle. Cut another semi-circle by inserting the cutter into hole 60. To cut out a D, repeat these steps on acid green paper, stopping 1/8 in. (3 mm) from the edge each time to create the vertical bar of the letter D. Glue the letters to the silver circle.

Cut with the circle-cutter

The circle-cutter is an instrument that allows one to cut circles with diameters of 1 to 16 in. (2.5 to 15 cm) easily. Place the tool on the material to cut, insert the point of the rotary cutter into one of the holes of the disk corresponding to the chosen diameter and rotate the disk 360° to cut your circle.

4 Form the Pockets

The pockets are made starting from a 4 1/2x6 in. (11.5x15 cm) rectangle. Score folds 1/2 in. (1.2 cm) from the two short sides and from one of the long sides. Cut the corners at 45°. The closure flaps are made starting with a 4 7/8 in. (12.3 cm) square. Score two folds 1/16 in. (2 mm) apart in the center of the square. Round the corners along one side of the square. Insert the flap into the pocket so that the final flap pocket is a 5 in. (12.5 cm) square. Secure the components to each other with tape. Apply glue to the small flaps. Adhere the pocket to a colored page leaving a 3/8 in. (1 cm) border all around. Glue a sticker to the flap pocket to represent a button. Follow the same steps to make another pocket and glue it 3/8 in. (1 cm) from the first. Place the two covers above and below the pages with the pockets. Insert the binder rings into the holes to complete the binder.

An Album-Game

Tools
- Pencil
- Eraser
- Ruler
- Utility knife
- Cutting mat
- Scissors
- Bone folder
- Animal stamps
- Black marker

Materials
- Fine-grained, felt-marked white card stock (125 g/m2)
- Scrapbooking paper with large letters
- Graph paper
- Six brush tip markers of different colors
- Black ink pad
- Colored stickers
- 10 in. (25 cm) of 1/8 in. (3 mm) wide satin ribbon
- 3/8 in. (1 cm) wide double-sided tape
- Glue dots

Diff./Time

Medium

1 hour and 30 min.

Have fun giving life to extraordinary creatures by building an album that pairs the heads, bodies and paws of different animals.

1 Cut the Paper

Cut out three 4 1/4x6 1/4 in. (11x16 cm) rectangles of card stock. Fold them in two to form three 3 1/8x6 1/4 in. (8x11 cm) cards. Cut out a 4 1/2x11 3/4 in. (11.5x30 cm) rectangle of patterned scrapbooking paper. Make reference lines 2 1/2 (6.6 cm) from the short sides. Using the bone folder, score folds in the center and along the reference lines. Fold to form a cover with two panels.

2 Draw the References

Draw a reference line 3/8 in. (1 cm) from the fold of each card. Using the bone folder, score the cards in along the lines. Open the cards and draw two lines parallel to the long sides, 1 1/2 in. (4 cm) from the edges. Cut the paper along the lines to the 3/8 in. (1 cm) margin. Refold the three panels to crispen the folds. Using a black marker, draw a 3 1/8x4 1/4 in. (8x11 cm) rectangle on the graph paper. Draw two parallel lines along the left side of the rectangle: one at 3/8 in. (1 cm) and one at 1 3/4 in. (4.5 cm).

IDEA. *You can make a hole in the album cover for tying the ribbon using a hand-held hole punch.*

4 Color the Animals

Color each animal with brush tip markers. Attach a colorful sticker at the top of each page.

3 Create the Animals

Draw a reference line in the center of the wood backing of each stamp. Ink the three stamps that form an animal and make some test stamps on scraps of white paper. Stamp each animal on a page cut into three.

5 Assemble the Album

Attach a strip of double-sided tape to each card along the fold. Overlay the three cards and press down well to make sure they adhere. Attach a strip of double-sided tape to the last card. Insert the assembled pages inside the cover flush with the fold and press down well. Place glue dots in the outer corners of the cover panels and fold them. Decorate the cover by tying a satin ribbon around the left edge of the album.

Stamp with Stamps

Position a card, closed, in the center of the graph paper. Ink the stamp and position it with the help of reference marks on the paper and on the wood backing. Stamp each part of the animal in the center of the three flaps (the head and the legs should be stamped along an edge, while the body in the center).

A Moroccan Album

Tools

- Pencil
- Ruler
- Utility knife
- Cutting mat
- Scissors
- Piercing tool
- Large needle with rounded tip

Materials

- Two dark blue-gray linear felt-marked A4 card stock (220 g/m2)
- Light blue-gray linear felt-marked A4 card stock (220 g/m2)
- Blue A4 card stock (220 g/m2)
- Gold A4 card stock
- Twelve sheets of A4 white paper (100 g/m2)
- Three sheets of A4 tracing paper
- White gold Precious Metal Effects Mouliné stranded cotton

Diff./Time

Easy

2 hours

Personalize the cover of your photo album with a geometrical design inspired by Moroccan tiles.

1 Prepare the Paper

Work with the sheets set horizontally. Trace the seamline 11 in. (28 cm) from the right edge of one of the light blue-green card stock sheets and on all of the light blue-gray, blue and gold sheets. All of the drawings will have to be centered in this 8 1/4x11 in. (21x28 cm) rectangle. Mark the center of the rectangle on each sheet. Copy the drawings onto three different sheets of tracing paper.

2 Trace the Motifs

Trace the drawings onto colored card stock: the red outline onto the dark blue-gray card stock, the blue onto the light blue-gray and the green onto the blue. Cut out the motifs using a utility knife. The gold card stock should not be cut.

IDEA. Make different gift albums by varying the colors of the card stock.

Create a Travel Album

Choose the decorations most representative of the country you visited. The design used in this project is inspired by Moroccan tiles, zellige, which are decorated with geometric designs. If you love drawing, painting, taking pictures or making collages, you could make the pages of this album from watercolor paper, black photo paper or tracing paper.

3 Make the Holes

Stack the sheets with the cutouts to make sure the motifs are centered perfectly. Overlay them in the following order: the gold sheet, the blue sheet, the light blue-gray sheet and finally, the dark blue-gray sheet. On the dark blue-gray cover, make a reference mark every 3/8 in. (1 cm) along the seam line. Using the piercing tool, make a hole in correspondance with the marks (use this sheet as a template for making holes in all the other color and white sheets).

4 Sew the Cover

After having made holes in all the sheets, overlay them remembering to place the second dark blue-gray sheet on the bottom. Prepare a long length of embroidery thread and tie a large knot at the end. Secure the album together by passing the gold thread through each hole. Once the sewing is done, finish with a knot and cut away excess thread.

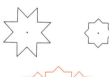

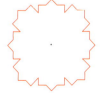

Enlarge the drawings by 560% in a photocopier.

Diagram for overlaying the cutouts.

25

The Golden Host's Book

Tools

- Pencil
- Ruler
- Utility knife
- Cutting mat
- Scissors
- Riveting kit

Materials

- 17 3/4x25 1/4 in. (45x64 cm) chipboard
- Forty white 10x7 in. (25x18 cm) sheets of paper
- Khaki linen paper
- A4 anise green natural paper
- A4 mauve paper
- Branch about 7 in. (18 cm) long and about 3/8 in. (1 cm) in diameter
- 4 in. (10 cm) long piece of thick white or ecru rubber band
- 11 3/4 in. (30 cm) of 3/16 in. (5 mm) wide mauve fabric ribbon
- Glue stick
- Spray adhesive

Diff./Time

Easy

1 hour

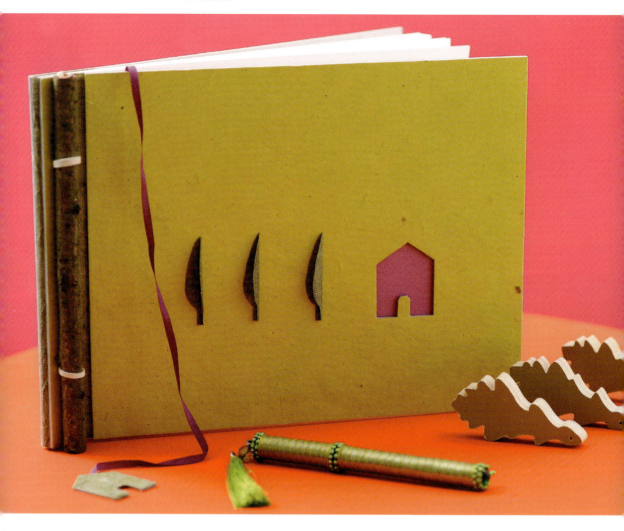

Made using natural materials, this album is equipped with a bookmark and is ready for the guests' anecdotes.

1 Cut the Components

Cut three rectangles from the chipboard: A – 8 7/8x7 in. (22.5x18 cm), B – 11/16x7 (1.7x18 cm) and C – 10x7 in. (25x18 cm). In rectangle A, incise a small house and set it aside. Cut a 4x7 in. (10x18 cm) strip of the khaki linen paper and an 8x7 in. (20x18 cm) rectangle of mauve paper.

2 Wrap the Cover

Spray rectangles A and B with spray adhesive. Glue them to the anise green natural paper. Trim the paper flush with the board (cut along the outline of the house as well). Spray the back of A with spray adhesive and adhere the mauve paper on top, aligning with the left edge of the rectangle.

Cut the Chipboard
Use a robust utility knife with a blade in 11/16 in. (18 mm) segments. Choose a model with an ergonomic holder and a safe lock system. While cutting, maintain a 90° angle between the blade and the cutting mat to avoid beveling the board.

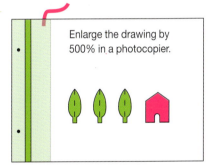

Enlarge the drawing by 500% in a photocopier.

3 Assemble

Glue rectangle A to the strip of khaki linen paper 1 in. (2.5 cm) from the right edge, inserting the ends of the mauve ribbon between the board and the paper. Glue B at 1 5/16 in. (3.3 cm) from the edge and C at 2 3/16 in. (5.5 cm). Using the punch (1/8 in. [3 mm] in diameter) and the hammer from the riveting kit, make holes where indicated in the drawing.

4 Insert the Pages

Insert the pages into the cover. Mark the locations of the holes. Remove the pages and punch holes in them. Replace the cover. Insert the rubber band into one hole from below, so that a loop, into which one end of the branch can be inserted, will appear above the cover. Pull on the rubber band, pass it through the second hole from below and insert the other end of the branch.

5 Decorate the Album

Reduce the size of the house slightly by cutting away 1/64 in. (0.5 mm) from each side until it easily fits into the opening in the cover. Using the glue stick, coat the house with khaki paper, inserting the other end of the mauve ribbon between the board and the paper.

THE CYPRESSES. Cut 3/4x2 in. (20x50 mm) rectangles of khaki linen paper. Fold them in two and shape with scissors by following the drawing. Open and glue just one half of the cypress trees onto the cover.

The Athlete's Album

Tools
- Pencil
- Precision knife
- Cutting mat
- Compass

Materials
- White watercolor paper
- Black corrugated paper
- Gray card stock
- Light and dark green card stock
- A4 light gray paper
- 8x8 in. (20x20 cm) spiral-bound album with a polypropylene cover
- Universal fast-drying adhesive
- Glue stick

Diff./Time

Easy

1 hour

A ball that peeks from behind blades of grass: now that is a suitable cover for an album of your favorite athletes' autographs.

28

1 Prepare the Support for the Cover

Cut out the grass following Drawing 1 (tall grass in light green, short grass in dark green). Extract the polypropylene cover from the album's spiral binding. Position it on top of the two shapes and cut the holes for the passage of the spiral. Glue the grass shapes one top of each other using the glue stick. Place the polypropylene cover on top of the light green card stock, trim the edges and cut the holes. Put the album back together, threading first the light green card stock then the polypropylene cover and then the grass onto the spiral.

Make the Holes

To thread the green card stock cover and both the grass shapes onto the album's cover without difficulty, use the polypropylene cover as a template for making the holes along the edges. Set it on top of the various card stock elements and cut out each hole with a utility knife. If the holes are round, you can use a hole punch, still employing the original cover as a reference.

Enlarge Drawing 2 by 400% in a photocopier.

Drawing 2

2 Cut Out the Ball

Cut out the hexagons (black and white) following Drawing 2: for those along the perimeter, add a 3/8 in. (1 cm) margin. Using the compass, draw two 8 in. (20 cm) circles on gray card stock and cut them out.

3 Glue the Hexagons

Photocopy Drawing 2 onto a sheet of light gray paper. Cut out the hexagon with the writing. Using the glue stick, adhere the three internal hexagons (white, black and light gray with writing) onto the circle of gray card stock leaving a space of about 1/32 in. (1 mm) in-between: use the hole made by the compass as a reference to help centering. Glue the other hexagons around the three central hexagons, continuing to leave a 1/32 in. (1 mm) space. Wait for the glue to dry and trim the hexagon edges extending beyond the circumference of the gray circle.

Enlarge Drawing 1 by 430% in a photocopier.

IDEA. You can cut out a photo of your favorite athlete and glue it to the center of the hexagon.

4 Glue the Circles

Glue the ball to the polypropylene cover. Attach the second gray circle to the back of the cover.

Drawing 1

Height 5 1/8 in. (13 cm)

A Priceless Herbarium

Tools

- Precision knife
- Cutting mat
- Alphabet stencil
- Pencil
- Decorative edge scissors, decker
- Leaves stamp

Materials

- 7x7 in. (18x18 cm) spiral note pad with light green pages
- A4 light blue paper
- A dried leaf
- Ink pads (three different shades of green)
- Dark green fine point marker
- Golden yellow marker
- 2 3/8 in. (6 cm) wide oval metal tag
- Two yellow paper fasteners
- One small perforated adhesive label
- 8 in. (20 cm) of silver string
- Universal fast-drying adhesive
- Double-sided tape
- Double-sided adhesive foam squares

Diff./Time

Easy

45 min.

On the pages of this notebook, you can gather the most beautiful leaves, embellishing them with text and original decorative elements.

1 Cut the Light Blue Paper

Position the leaf so its edge aligns with the right edge of the light blue paper. Trace its outline with a pencil. Cut along the outline with a precision knife leaving the corner of the page intact.

2 Make the Labels and the Border

Tear one page out of the pad. Set the metal tag on top and trace its inner and outer edges with a pencil. Using the stencil, write the name of the plant with the dark green marker. Cut out the oval and glue it in the lower right corner of the light blue paper with the leaf shape. Place the metal tag on top and mark the location of the two holes. Make incisions at the reference marks with the knife. Secure the metal tag to the page with the paper fasteners. Color the adhesive label with the golden yellow marker, and write the place and date where the leaf was gathered with the dark green marker. Tear out one more page from the pad and stamp it with the leaves motif along two perpendicular sides.

3 Compose the Page

In the lower right corner of the note pad's right page, glue the light blue paper with the leaf. Attach the leaf on top using pieces of double-sided tape, offsetting it a bit with respect to its silhouette. Thread the silver string through the label and glue it to the back of the border. Attach the border to the upper left corner and the label between the leaf and the border using foam pads.

Make the Decorative Border

Stamp the leaves motif along one side of the green page continuing along the adjacent side (use two or three different shades of green for the motifs). Allow to dry. Cut out the border about 1/8 in. (4 mm) from the leaves leaving the external edges of the page untouched.

4 Write the Text

Compose the text on the computer and print it on light blue paper. Draw a margin 1 1/4 in. (3 cm) from the text and cut it out with decorative edge scissors. Attach the text to the pad's left page using four double-sided adhesive foam squares.

SUGGESTION.
In the text on the left, you can talk about when you gathered the leaf or the botanical properties of the plant.

The Trompe-l'œil Album

Tools

- Pencil ▸ Ruler ▸ Triangle ruler ▸ Cutting mat ▸ Utility knife ▸ Scissors
- Decorative edge scissors
- Bone folder
- Calligraphy pen
- Fine sandpaper
- Round-tipped paintbrush
- Flat-tipped paint brush

Materials

- 6x8 in. (15.1x20.5 cm) photo album to cover ▸ Two A4 foam board sheets, 1/8 in. (3 mm) thick ▸ A4 white card stock
- 9x21 in. (23x53 cm) light wood-patterned scrapbooking paper
- Photographs
- White adhesive label
- Black caligraphy ink
- Black pencil
- Acrylic paint: red, yellow ocher, lemon yellow, white, black
- Correction pen ▸ Masking tape ▸ Repositionable spray adhesive ▸ Elmer's glue ▸ Glue stick

Diff./Time

Difficult

2 hours
Drying time: one day

Put your skill to the test by making this album with decorations created with strokes of acrylic paint.

32

1 Cut the Components

Cut two 6 1/2x8 3/16 in. (16.3x20.8 cm) rectangles in the foam board. Cut one 6 3/8x1 1/2 in. (16.1x3.8 cm) rectangle (the spine) in the card stock. Check that the sides are perpendicular. Smooth the edges of the foam board with the sandpaper.

4 Paint the Stripes

Using the correction pen, draw lines parallel to the ribbons, 4 in. (10 cm) apart. Using the black pencil, draw black lines below the white, to create a shadow.

Paint the Details

Paint the nails using a piece of paper with a hole as a template. Using the flat-tipped paintbrush, paint a yellow ochre background. Using the round-tipped paintbrush, color 1/3 with yellow ochre darkened with a touch of black, and 1/3 with yellow ochre lightened with a touch of lemon yellow. Finish with a point of lemon yellow and white. Draw a fly on the spine using black and white acrylic paint and a black pencil (use the drawing as inspiration).

2 Wrap the Cover

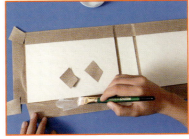

Place the light wood-patterned scrapbooking paper on the working surface with the back facing up. Brush glue onto the card stock rectangle (the spine) and glue it to the center of the paper. Brush glue onto the foam board rectangles and glue them on either side of the spine, 1/8 in. (3 mm) away. Turn over and gently smooth the surface to remove any air bubbles. Turn over again and cut away the corners of the paper about 1/8 in. (3 mm) from the outer corners of the foam board rectangles. Brush the glue onto the paper flaps and fold them using the bone folder so they adhere well to the foam board. Allow to dry.

5 Paint the Silhouette

Write the text on the adhesive label using the calligraphy pen and black ink. Photocopy the photos and cut out the subjects to create templates. Cut out card stock rectangles of the same size as the photos. Spray the back of the templates with repositionable spray adhesive and adhere to the card stock. Coat with gray paint (white plus black) using a dry flat-tipped paintbrush. Allow to dry. Remove the templates. Cut the borders with decorative-edge scissors leaving a white margin.

3 Paint the Ribbons

Turn the cover over once more. Attach a strip of masking tape parallel to the right short side, 1/2 in. (1.2 cm) from the edge; leave a 3/8 in. (8 mm) space and attach another strip of tape. Attach a strip of tape 7 1/4 in. (18.5 cm) from the right edge; leave a 3/8 in. (8 mm) space and attach another strip. Attach a strip of tape parallel to the left short side, 3 1/2 in. (9 cm) from the edge; leave a 3/8 in. (8 mm) space and attach another strip. Brush on undiluted red acrylic paint with a flat-tipped paintbrush. Similarly, mask off and paint two strips 1/2 in. (1.2 cm) from the horizontal sides and one diagonal strip. Underline one edge of the ribbons to create a shadow. Add touches of pink (white plus red) to soften the red at the intersections.

6 Decorate the Album

Attach the adhesive label to the cover, cutting away the sections that would cover the ribbons. Proceed in the same way with the silhouettes, gluing them with the glue stick. Using the black pencil, draw a nail and its shadow straddling the edge of one of the silhouettes (using the round-tipped paintbrush, add a point of white). Glue the spine of the cover to that of the album using Elmer's glue.

TRICK. To reinforce the cover, cut out and glue an endpaper at the beginning and at the end of the album.

The Wedding Album

Tools
- Pencil ▸ Eraser ▸ Ruler
- Utility knife ▸ Rotary cutter
- Cutting mat ▸ Template for cutting concentric circles
- Template for cutting concentric ovals ▸ Scissors
- Two pairs of decorative edge scissors: long (8 in., 20 cm) and short (5 1/4 in., 13.5 cm) ▸ Round corner craft punch ▸ Decorative corner craft punch ▸ Bone folder ▸ Cursive writing stamp

Materials
- White paper with silver motifs ▸ Roll of white Kraft paper ▸ White card stock (224 g/m2)
- Natural paper: white, classic and with small holes
- White transluscent paper with white printed motifs
- White tissue paper ▸ Copy paper ▸ White adhesive mesh ▸ Round paper doilies ▸ Cardboard letters ▸ Colored photos ▸ Paper flowers ▸ Small 3D adhesive flowers ▸ Fabric flowers ▸ White paper fasteners ▸ Mother-of-pearl button ▸ 23 1/2 in. (60 cm) of 3/16 in. (5 mm) wide white satin ribbon ▸ Gold ink pad ▸ Double-sided tape ▸ 3/4 in. (2 cm) wide masking tape ▸ Clear glue dots
- Universal fast-drying adhesive ▸ Spray adhesive

Diff./Time

Difficult

4 hours

Explanation on 2 spreads

Delicate lace, transparencies and natural papers characterize this album commemorating an unforgettable day!

PREPARATION OF THE ALBUM

1 Cut the Pages

From the white card stock, obtain two 6x8 1/4 in. (15x21 cm) rectangles A (the cover), five 5 3/4x8 1/4 in. (14.6x21 cm) rectangles B, and six 4 1/2x8 1/4 in. (11.5x21 cm) rectangles C (internal pages; one rectangle C will be used to decorate the cover). Place one rectangle B and one C next to each other and join them with a strip of masking tape. Trim the masking tape flush with the paper. Repeat for rectangles B and C.

TRICK. *Use a strip of Kraft paper about the same length as the pages that will comprise your album.*

2 Make the Accordion Fold

Cut an 8 1/4 in. (21 cm) wide strip of white Kraft paper the length of your roll. Make reference marks 5/8 in. (1.5 cm) apart along the long sides with a pencil.

Make the Pleating

Align the ruler with the reference marks and score the folds with a bone folder. Accordion fold by alternating valley and mountain folds.

3 Perforate the Corners

Perforate the upper right corner of each B+C rectangle pair using the decorative corner craft punch and trim the bottom right corner with the rounded corner craft punch. Cut the long side of rectangles C with the short decorative edge scissors.

4 Glue the Photo to the Cover

Cut two 8 1/4 in. (21 cm) squares from silver patterned white paper. Fold along one of the long sides of each at 2 3/8 in. (6 cm). Reopen the squares and coat the back with spray adhesive. Glue the sheets to rectangles A folding the 2 3/8 in. (6 cm) flap around the edges. From the remaining rectangle C, cut a circle with a diameter of 3 3/4 in. (9.5 cm) centered along the width and 3/8 in. (1 cm) from the bottom using the template for cutting concentric circles and a rotary cutter. Cut a circle with a diameter of 3 3/8 in. (8.5 cm) from a photo. Glue it to a doily and attach to the back of rectangle C with masking tape.

5 Create the Text

Place the cardboard letters onto a white sheet. Ink the cursive writing stamp with an ink pad. Press the stamp against the letters. Allow to dry. Type the text on the computer using a fantasy font. Print the text onto a white sheet of paper 3/4 in. (2 cm) from the left edge.

DECORATION OF THE PAGES

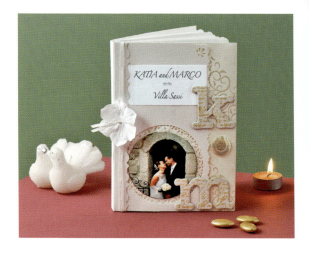

1 Glue the Paper Components

Prepare the coverings for the three rectangles B by cutting out one rectangle from translucent paper, one from classic natural paper and one from tissue paper with the same dimensions as B. Attach the decorative paper onto rectangles B using glue dots. Cut one rectangle from natural paper with small holes and one from the mesh with the same width as rectangles B but an inferior height (choose the height you prefer). Attach the natural paper rectangle with holes using glue dots. Remove the protective backing from the mesh and attach it. Cut a rectangle of paper with silver motifs and glue it to rectangle C using spray adhesive.

2 Cut the Photos

Using the templates for cutting concentric circles and ovals and a rotary cutter, make some portrait holes in rectangles C. Cut some photos in the same way: position the template over the photo and shift it to find the best view, then incise with the rotary cutter. Use the decorative corner craft punch to perforate the corners of the square and rectangular photographs. Using double-sided tape, attach the photos to rectangles B. Secure the photos below the portrait holes using masking tape.

IDEA. Choose papers in different hues of white, with different weights and textures. Overlay, cut and tear them to create different effects!

3 Decorate the Pages

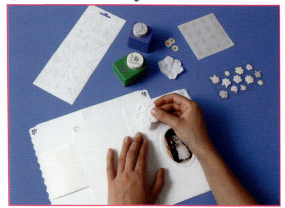

Let your creativity run wild decorating the album's cover and internal pages. Secure the fabric flowers with white paper fasteners (make a small incision with a utility knife so you can insert the paper fasteners). Attach the paper flowers with a drop of fast-drying adhesive, and the 3D adhesive flowers. Fold and glue the B+C rectangle pairs together with four glue dots positioned in the corners of C, so that the tape holding the rectangles together remains on the inside.

ASSEMBLING THE ALBUM

1 Mount the Pages

Glue the album pages to the folds in the plated paper: glue the first page inside the second valley fold by applying a line of fast-drying adhesive on both faces of the fold. Press together well to secure the page. Glue the other pages in the same manner, skipping a fold between each page (insert a white piece of paper below the fold being glued to avoid stains). When all the pages are attached, leave one extra fold and cut off the rest of the plated paper. Fold the unused Kraft paper folds towards the exterior and glue together around the back.

SUGGESTION. Decide the order of the pages based on the chosen photos: entrance into the church or city hall, exit, witnesses, family, cocktails etc.

2 Glue the Cover

Deposit a line of fast-drying adhesive in the first valley fold. Insert rectangle A, refold the Kraft paper and press together well. Repeat for the back cover. Glue a strip of white paper with silver motifs between the cover and the first page to hide the Kraft paper.

IDEA. Make a bookmark using a white satin ribbon.

3 Bind the Album

Cut two 1 3/8x8 1/4 in. (3.5x21 cm) strips from white card stock. Shape the right edge of both strips with long decorative-edge scissors. Draw a reference line 5/8 in. (1.5 cm) from the straight edge. Using the bone folder, score a fold along this line. Fold the flap. Glue the strip to the cover such that the shaped edge partially covers the rectangle with the text and the circle with the photo (don't glue down the flap). Repeat for the second strip on the back. Fold and glue the two flaps to form a spine.

4 Decorate the Cover

Using adhesive spray, attach the rectangle with the text to the back of the remaining rectangle C, and both onto the front cover. Glue the cardboard letters and the button using fast-drying adhesive. Tie the white satin ribbon around the front cover.

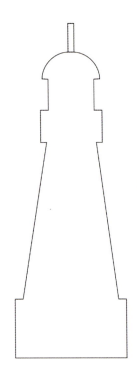

Notebooks, Pads and Address Books

A Blue and Gold Notebook

Tools

- Utility knife
- Cutting mat
- Ruler
- Scissors
- Rotary cutter
- Compass with adaptor
- Needle
- Two paper clamps

Materials

- 10x12 1/2 in. (25x32 cm) blue natural paper
- 9x11 3/4 in. (23x30 cm) light blue paper (160 g/m2)
- Paper scraps in shades of blue (patterned and solid)
- Gold paper scraps
- Twelve A4 sheets of paper
- A4 white translucent paper
- Two 9 1/2 in. (24 cm) of 3/8 in. (1 cm) wide blue satin ribbons
- Blue and white sewing thread
- Glue stick

Diff./Time

Easy

1 hour

No one will remain indifferent faced with these notebooks of abstract motifs, as sophisticated in appearance as they are simple to create!

1 Cut the Paper

Cut a 2 3/8 in. (6 cm) circle of light blue paper and a 4 in. (10 cm) semicircle of the patterned paper in shades of blue. Obtain a 6 3/4x4 1/4 in. (17x11 cm) rectangle of patterned paper in shades of blue, a small square of blue natural paper and a rectangle of patterned paper in tones of blue by tearing the edges. From the gold paper, tear a 13 1/2 in. (34 cm) long strip and cut a strip 3/8 in. (1 cm) wide and 13 1/2 in. (34 cm) long. Cut a strip of light blue patterned paper (3/8x13 1/2 in. [1x34 cm]), and tear a strip of sky blue natural paper (5/8x13 1/2 in. [1.5x34 cm]).

2 Compose the Cover

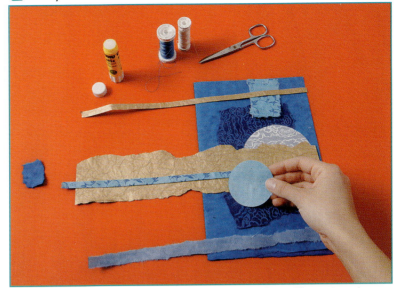

Fold the sheet of blue natural paper in half and set it on the working surface. Arrange the decorations on top as you prefer: start by positioning the large rectangle, the semicircle and the wider gold strip, then arrange the circle, the small rectangles and the remaining strips. Sew the paper components folding any excess over the edge.

3 Glue the Endpaper

Position the 9x11 3/4 in. (23x30 cm) light blue paper on the back of the cover. Glue the ribbons between the sheets in the middle of the page, on the left and on the right. Glue down the light blue paper.

Sew the Paper

After having decided on the composition, move the pieces of paper to the working surface arranging them in the same pattern. Secure the rectangle of dark blue paper to the open cover with a few drops of glue. Set the sewing machine to 3 and the running stich. Sew the paper shapes about 1/8 in. (3 mm) from the edge with blue thread. Cut the threads 4 in. (10 cm) from the last stitch and pass them to the back using a needle to tie. Attach the various pieces to the cover one by one with drops of glue and sew (for the narrower strips, stitch just one central line).

4 Insert the Pages

Fold the twelve white paper sheets in half. Fold the translucent paper in half. Insert the white sheets into the translucent white paper. Mark the fold in the sheets. Trim the paper along three of the sides. Open the sheets and set them against the fold, inside the cover. Fix them with paper clamps. Insert a spool of white thread into the sewing machine. Sew the pages and the cover together along the fold with a running stitch set to 4. Make one or two holes to tie the threads. Pass the threads to the inside of the notebook with a needle, tie and cut. Tie the ribbons.

TRICK. *If your compass does not have an adaptor, cut the circles using a template for cutting concentric circles.*

The Lighthouse Notebook

Tools
- Pencil
- Ruler
- Utility knife
- Cutting mat
- Bone folder
- Flat-tipped paintbrush
- Small diameter hole punch

Materials
- A4 blue card stock
- A4 watercolor paper
- Five sheets of A4 white paper
- Blue and red acrylic paint
- 3 ft (1 m) of dark blue string
- A small white stone
- Universal fast-drying adhesive

Diff./Time

Easy

1 hour

Nothing is better than this fun booklet with a lighthouse on the cover to record memories of your beach vacation!

1 Cut

From each sheet of paper, cut an 8 1/4 in. (21 cm) square. Using the tip of the bone folder, score along the center of the sheets and fold them. Transfer the drawing of the lighthouse to the blue card stock and cut it out.

2 Paint the Lines

On one half of the watercolor paper, draw faint lines with a pencil, following the diagram. Color between the lines with acrylic paint.

3 Make the Holes

Fold the watercolor paper in half and make a hole half-way along the fold using a hole punch (center the hole punch on the fold). Due the same for the blue card stock. Insert the watercolor paper into the blue card stock so the lines are visible through the lighthouse cutout. Punch holes in the other white sheets and insert them into the cover aligning the holes perfectly.

Tips for Painting the Lines

Dilute a little bit of blue acrylic paint with water. Paint the lines with a flat-tipped paintbrush and allow to dry. Dilute a small amount of red acrylic paint and paint the line as shown on the diagram. If you prefer more intense colors, allow to dry and apply one or two more coats of paint. If the watercolor paper deform while drying (depending on the weight of the paper and the water contents of the paint), cover it with a cloth and smooth with a warm iron.

4 Insert the String

Pass one end of the string through the holes from the inside of the fold. Pass the other end over the top of the album and insert it into the hole. Now, pass it over the bottom towards the other end of the string.

5 Secure the Stone

Tie the two ends of the string together. Wrap the stone with the string and make two very tight knots. Trim any white paper protruding from the edges of the notebook with a utility knife.

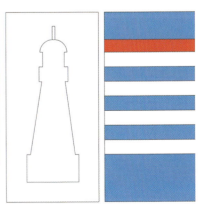

Enlarge the two diagrams by 240% in a photocopier.

TRICK. *You can glue the string to the stone for better stability.*

43

A Woven Cover

Tools

- Utility knife
- Decorative edge scissors, zig zag
- Ruler
- Cutting mat
- Clear tape
- Removable tape
- Glue stick

Materials

- A color magazine page in tones of green
- A4 sheets of burgundy, red and lilac paper

Diff./Time

Easy

1 hour

Personalize your notebook with this fun cover made by weaving together strips of color paper.

1 Cut the Strips of Paper

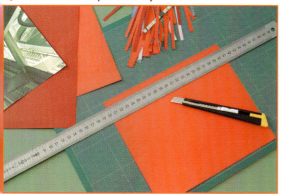

Cut some 3/16, 3/8 and 3/4 in. (0.5, 1 and 2 cm) wide strips from color paper and the magazine page. Use the lines on the cutting mat as guides to make sure the cuts are parallel.

2 Weave the Strips Together

Use some pieces of removable tape to fix the strips vertically one next the other on the cutting mat for a length slightly greater than that of the notebook. Weave in the horizontal strips: pass them over one vertical strip and under the next. Continue alternating the over and under steps.

3 Shape the Border

Attach strips of clear tape along the edges of the woven rectangle, on both the back and the front. Cut the edges with decorative edge scissors along the center of the tape.

Play with the Colored Strips!
Make a checkered pattern alternating the different colors at will. The originality of this design is partly due to the addition of strips cut from color magazines: you can easily find a page in shades of green (in advertisements or gardening articles). For this project, 3/16, 3/8 and 3/4 in. (0.5, 1 and 2 cm) red strips, 3/16 and 3/8 in. (0.5 and 1 cm) burgundy strips, 3/16 in. (0.5 cm) lilac strips and 3/16 in. (0.5 cm) green strips were used.

4 Glue the Cover

Open the notebook cover. Coat the cover of the notebook with glue using a glue stick. Take the woven rectangle and adhere it to the cover pressing down firmly with your hands.

TRICK. After covering the notebook, apply a little bit of glue to the ends of the strips to secure them.

The Fall Note Pad

Tools

- B hardness pencil
- Scissors
- Decoupage scissors
- Repositionable spray adhesive
- Tracing paper
- Card stock
- Shoebox
- Calligraphy pen
- Color markers

Materials

- A pad with a window
- Yellow, orange, red and brown natural paper

Diff./Time

Easy

1 hour and 30 min.

Decorated with leaves of warm fall colors, this graceful note pad will jealously guard your thoughts and your notes.

1 Make the Templates

Trace the outlines of the leaves onto tracing paper with a pencil. Turn it over and set on the card stock. Retrace the outlines with a pencil to transfer the outlines. Cut out the two motifs following the lines carefully.

2 Cut Out the Leaves

Set the two templates on each sheet of color paper and trace their outlines with a pencil. Cut out the traced motifs using decoupage scissors.

Enlarge the drawings of the leaves by 200% in a photocopier.

3 Modify the Hues

If the color of the paper seems too light, color the inside of the leaf with a marker of the same color to obtain a bolder hue.

4 Glue

Spray the spray adhesive onto one side of the cut-out leaves. Glue the leaves to the cover of the note pad around the opening, alternating the colors. Write the word "leaves" with a calligraphy pen inside the square that you will have drawn on the first inside page, in correspondance with the note pad opening.

Assemble Using Spray Adhesive

To avoid getting glue on your working surface, place the motifs on the bottom of a shoebox while applying the spray adhesive. Hold the can at a distance of about a foot (30 cm) while spraying, allow to sit for 2 minutes, lift the leaves and transfer to a piece of paper. Take the leaves one at a time and adhere to the cover of the note pad.

47

Poppies on a Notebook

Tools

- Pencil
- Ruler
- Utility knife
- Cutting mat
- Scissors
- Piercing tool
- Hand-held hole punch 1/8 in. [3 mm] in diameter

Materials

- 6 1/2x8 3/4 in. (16.5x22 cm) notebook
- A4 white card stock
- A4 red paper
- Red tissue paper
- Patterned scrapbooking paper with small leaves
- Patterned scrapbooking paper with colored stripes
- Patterned scrapbooking paper with flowers over a light background
- Green marker
- Black marker
- Two small anise green paper fasteners
- Glue stick

Diff./Time

Easy

45 min.

Create a floral cover with two poppies in the foreground for a notebook intended for safekeeping gardening secrets.

1 Cut the Paper

Trim the notebook until it is a 6 1/2 in. (16.5 cm) square. Cut a square of the same size from the floral scrapbooking paper. Cut a 3 1/8x6 1/2 in. (8x16.5 cm) rectangle from the striped scrapbooking paper. Cut a 2x6 1/2 in. (5x16.5 cm) rectangle from the scrapbooking paper with leaves.

2 Compose the Text

Type the title on the computer using a black fantasy font. Print on red paper. Cut out the writing forming a strip 6 1/2 in. (16.5 cm) long and no wider than 3/8 in. (1 cm). From the red paper, cut a 10 1/4x6 1/2 in. (26.2x16.5 cm) rectangle.

Enlarge the drawings by 295% in a photocopier.

IDEA. *Discolor the tissue paper using a marker soaked in diluted bleach: this will make the flower look like a buttercup or an anemone.*

3 Prepare the Template

Photocopy the petal template and the leaf illustration onto white card stock. Cut out the petal and the leaves with scissors.

4 Assemble

Glue the 10 1/4x6 1/2 in. (26.2x16.5 cm) red paper rectangle to the back of the notebook. To the cover of the notebook, glue the floral square followed by the striped rectangle flush with the lower edge; then glue the rectangle with the leaves over the previous rectangle, also flush with the lower edge. Glue the strip with the text flush with the upper side of the rectangle with leaves. Glue the drawing of the leaves flush with the upper edge of the striped rectangle, slightly offset to the right. Using the punch, make a hole in the cover above the drawing of the leaves and to the left, almost flush with the spine. Insert the tabs of the paper fasteners into the holes and spread the tabs flat to secure the flowers. Cut the petals of the poppy on the left flush with the spine.

Make the Poppies

Cut eight 3 1/8x2 3/8 in. (8x6 cm) rectangles from red tissue paper. Stack the rectangles, place the petal template on top and trace the edge with a pencil. Hold the tissue paper rectangles between your fingers and cut along the outline with scissors. Using the hand-held hole punch, make a hole in the petals as indicated on the template. Crumple the petals a bit then smooth them once more. Overlay four petals lining up the holes and join them with a small paper fastener. Rotate the petals around this axis. Using the green marker, draw a shadow around the paper fastener and using the black, draw the pistils. Repeat for the other poppy.

49

The Secret Diary

Tools

- Ruler ▸ Utility knife
- Cutting mat
- Glue stick
- Removable tape
- Three stamps (star, flower and heart)
- Ink pads
- Pink glitter glue pen
- Black marker

Materials

- A small notebook
- An A4 sheet of pink paper
- An A4 sheet of fuchsia paper
- Two gummed cloth picture hangers
- A small lock
- Adhesive letters

Diff./Time

Easy

30 min.

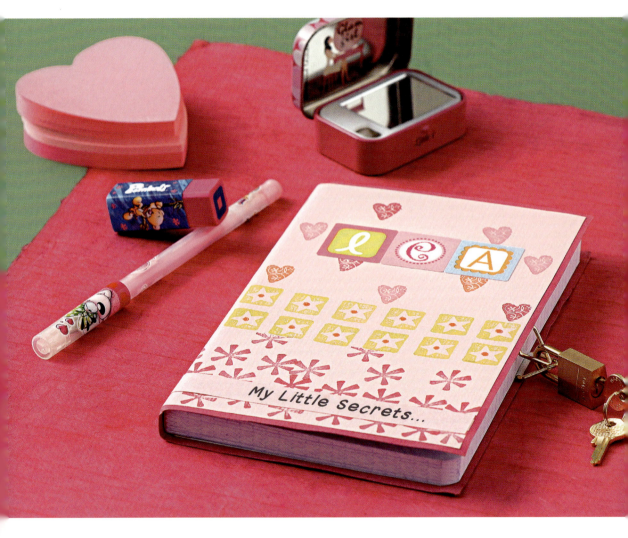

Nothing is better than this pink diary decorated with stamps and closed with a golden lock for safeguarding your secrets!

50

1 Prepare the Cover

Draw and cut a 6 7/8x9 1/2 in. (17.6x24 cm) rectangle from the A4 fuchsia paper, a 6 3/4x9 1/4 in. (17x23.4 cm) rectangle from the A4 pink paper and a 1/2x9 1/4 in. (1.2x23.4 cm) strip from pink scraps.

2 Stamp the Stars

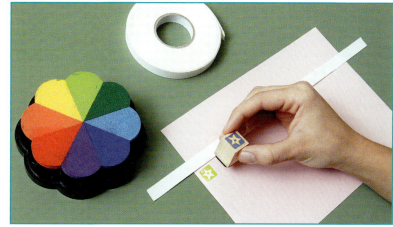

Position a piece of removable tape to the pink paper. Decorate the sheet with a double row of stars, inking the stamp before each use.

3 Stamp Flowers and Hearts

Remove the removable tape and stamp flowers and hearts following your sense of aesthetics, on either side of the double line of stars. Practice on a sheet of paper before starting. Once the motifs are dry, compose the name using adhesive letters.

Mark Off the Area to be Stamped

The double row of stars should be oriented horizontally with respect to the long sides of the pink sheet. Attach a strip of removable tape 2 3/16 in. (5.5 cm) from the bottom of the sheet to guide you. You can also draw faint reference lines with a pencil. Once the motifs are stamped, allow the ink to dry and gently erase the reference lines with an eraser.

4 Secure the Hangers

To ensure the diary remains "truly" secret, you will need to add a closure: moisten the gummed cloth of the cloth picture hangers and secure them to the inside of the booklet, halfway along each cover (let the metal triangles protrude beyond the edges).

5 Glue the Cover

Using the glue stick, glue the pink sheet to the center of the fuchsia sheet. Attach the strip 3/8 in. (1 cm) from the edge of the pink sheet. Glue the result to the booklet and smooth well with your hands. Write the diary's title in the center of the closed cover with a black marker. Close the diary with the lock.

TRICK. Decorate the center of each star using a glitter glue pen.

A Pocket Note Pad

Tools
- Pencil
- Ruler
- Utility knife
- Cutting mat
- Scissors
- Bone folder

Materials
- 3x4 in. (7.5x10.5 cm) pad
- A4 ecru paper
- A4 turquoise paper
- Circle-patterned scrapbooking paper
- Letter stamp
- Red ink pad
- Turquoise sewing thread
- Glue stick
- Removable tape
- Adhesive tape

Diff./Time

Medium

1 hour

Elegance and originality set apart this note pad cover personalized with your initials.

1 Prepare the Cover

Cut two rectangles from the ecru paper: one 9x3 3/8 in. (23x8.5 cm) and one 1 1/2x3 in. (4x7.5 cm). Cut three rectangles from the turquoise paper: one 9x3 3/8 in. (23x8.5 cm) and two 1 1/2x3 3/8 in. (4x8.5 cm). Cut a strip that includes four circles from the scrapbooking paper. Using scissors, round off one of the ends of the strip cutting along the outline of a circle.

2 Make the Guide

Glue the two 9x3 3/8 in. (23x8.5 cm) rectangles, the turquoise and the ecru, together. Using the bone folder, score one fold at 4 1/4 in. (11 cm) and another at 4 3/4 in. (12 cm) from a short edge, obtaining a 1/2 in. (1 cm) spine. Set the rectangle on the cutting mat with the turquoise side facing up. Make two pencil lines parallel to the short side: one at 5/8 in. (1.5 cm) from the edge and the other at 1 1/4 in. (3 cm). Measure the width of the scrapbooking paper strip (here 1 in. [2.4 cm]) to determine the location of the incisions. Make pencil lines 1 1/4 in. (3 cm) from the long sides. Using a utility knife, make two incisions (here, 5/8 in. [1.5 cm] long) parallel to the long sides in correspondance to the intersections of the pencil lines. Fold the 1 1/2x3 in. (4x7.5 cm) rectangles into three equal parts lengthwise (ecru side on the outside). Insert the ends into the incisions from the ecru side of the rectangle. Fold them towards each other on the back and overlap. Secure them with adhesive tape.

3 Assemble the Components

Center and secure the strip of scrapbooking paper 1 in. (2.5 cm) from the side opposite the side with the guide (the side with the circles should face down) with a piece of removable tape. Attach the two 1 1/2x3 3/8 in. (4x8.5 cm) rectangles to either end of the cover (with the turquoise side facing up, like that of the cover) with removable tape. Sew all around with turquoise thread starting from the short sides. Stamp the name initials in the center of one of the circles.

TRICK.
To reinforce the strip of scrapbooking paper, before cutting, you can back with a strip of clear self-adhesive plastic.

Sew the Note Pad Cover
Sew the edges of the cover with a running stich on a sewing machine, 1/8 in. (4 mm) from the edge. You can use the zigzag stitch, or sew several crossing parallel lines.

4 Insert the Note Pad

Insert the note pad into the small pockets sewn to the inside of the cover.

Sea-colored Note Pads

Tools
- Pencil
- Ruler
- Utility knife
- Cutting mat
- Scissors
- Needle
- Piercing tool
- Paper clamp

Materials
- Blue, light blue and white natural paper
- Unbleached recycled paper
- White paper scraps
- Embroidery thread or string
- Glass beads and shells

Diff./Time

Easy

45 min.

Construct these charming recycled paper booklets bound with string and decorated with beads and shells.

1 Cut the Paper

Cut an 8 3/4x2 3/4 in. (22x7 cm) rectangle of natural paper (cover). Cut sixteen 8 1/2x2 3/4 in. (21x7 cm) rectangles of recycled paper (pages) and fold them in half. On a piece of white paper with a 2 3/4 in. (7 cm) side (piercing template), draw a line 3/8 in. (1 cm) from the edge, and make four marks 1/2 in. (1.4 cm) apart.

2 Pierce the Paper

Position the piercing template on top of the pages and pierce with a piercing tool in correspondance with the marks. Stack the pages and set the cover on top. Place the template on top of the cover. Secure together with a paper clamp. Pierce with a piercing tool. Remove the template. Secure once more with the clamp.

IDEA. By modifying the dimensions and type of paper used, the spaces between stitches, the color of the thread and the decorations, you can create different note pads suited to any occasion!

3 Sew (1)

Thread about 20 in. (50 cm) of thread into a needle and pass it (from above) into the second hole. Insert the needle into the first hole (from below). Pass the thread over the spine and insert into the first hole once more. Pass it over the side of the album and into the first hole.

4 Sew (2)

Pass the needle through the second hole (from above), through the third hole (from below) and into the fourth hole (from above). Remove the paper clamp. Pass the thread around the spine (from below). Pass it over the edge of the album (from above) and insert into the fourth hole.

5 Decorate the Thread

Continue to sew until you end up in the hole you started with. Knot the two ends of the thread. Thread the beads (or the shells) onto the threads securing them with a knot. Cut the threads to the same length and fray the ends.

Choose the Binding Thread

You can sew the note pad with kitchen twine, hemp twine or embroidery thread of the same hue as the natural paper. Choose the size of the holes based on the diameter of the thread (consider that the thread will be passed three times through each hole).

The Faux Leather Cover

Tools

- Yellow pencil
- Ruler
- Utility knife
- Cutting mat
- Scissors
- Bone folder
- Hatpin

Materials

- 25 1/2x40 in. (65x100 cm) sheet of olive green faux leather paper
- Havanna Kraft paper
- 6x8 1/4 in. (15x21 cm) notebook
- Pen
- Metal decorations: corners, paper fasteners and a washer
- 3/16 in. (5 mm) wide double-sided tape
- Glue dots
- Elmer's glue with dispenser cap

Diff./Time

Medium

2 hours and 30 min.

Your diary or phone book will acquire a refined look if you wrap it with a faux leather cover.

1 Cut the Cover

Transfer the diagram onto Kraft paper. Cut a 10x18 1/2 in. (25x47 cm) rectangle of faux leather paper and mark the locations of the folds and the flaps.

Cut and Fold the Faux Leather Paper

Position the Kraft paper template on the back of the faux leather paper. Using the yellow pencil, draw the flaps and mark the location of the folds (dashed lines). Using the utility knife, make oblique cuts around the flaps to eliminate the areas shown in gray on the diagram. Score the dashed lines with a bone folder. Fold all the flaps C and D towards the back. Insert the notebook into the cover and test the folding.

2 Fold the Cover

Apply Elmer's glue to the back of flaps C and D, and adhere them to the cover pressing down for a few moments. Do the same with flaps A. Apply Elmer's glue over flaps C. Fold flaps B towards the inside and adhere them to flaps A to form pockets.

3 Make the Strip

Cut a 7/8x7 3/4 in. (2x19 cm) strip of faux leather paper and fold it in half. Insert the pen inside the strip to determine the diameter needed for the loop. Brush Elmer's glue inside the strip, leaving the portion of the paper needed to hold the pen free of glue.

4 Glue the Strip

Brush Elmer's glue onto the back of the folded strip. Glue the strip to B, centering along height (fold and glue any excess below B). Make sure the loop extends beyond the outer edge of B. Insert the pen into the loop. With your hand inside the pocket, pierce the ends of the strip with the hatpin and insert a small paper fastener.

5 Apply the Decorations

Place some double-sided tape on the back of the metal corners and attach them close to the corners of the cover. Insert a large paper fastener into the washer. Using a glue dot, attach the washer close to the outer edge of the cover, centering along height. Insert the notebook cover inside the pockets of the faux leather cover.

A "Precious" Address Book

Tools
- Pencil
- Ruler
- Utility knife
- Cutting mat
- Flat-tipped paintbrush
- Bone folder

Materials
- 6 1/2x4 3/4 in. (16.5x12 cm) address book
- A4 bronze metallic paper
- A4 gold metallic paper
- Gold leaf
- Adhesive letters
- Two bronze metal beads with a large hole
- 13 3/4 in. (35 cm) of 3/16 in (5 mm) bronze ribbon
- Water-based gilding size
- Elmer's glue

Diff./Time

Difficult

1 hour

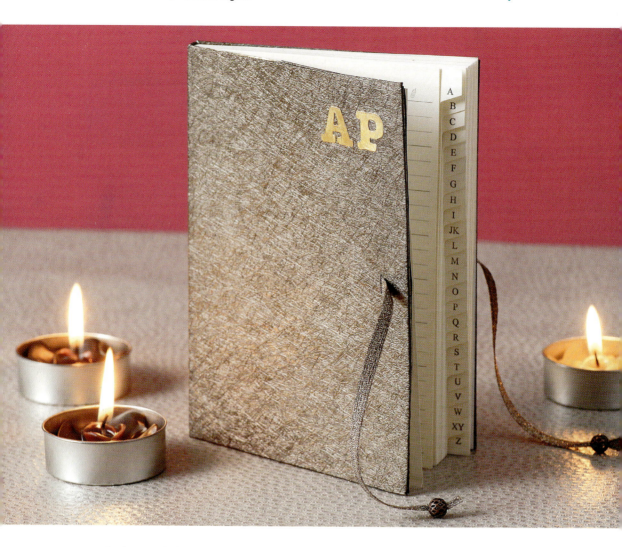

Adorn this purse-sized address book by covering it with glittering paper and adding gilded initials!

1 Cut the Cover

From the bronze metallic paper, cut an 8 1/8x11 in. (20.5x38 cm) rectangle. Set the closed address book on the back of the rectangle with only the spine touching and center it. Make reference marks. Open the first page and trace its outline with a pencil. Do the same for the last page. Cut the paper to the reference line in correspondance with the spine reference marks, obtaining two small isosceles trapezoids. Also, make 45° cuts at the corners about 1/8 in. (3 mm) from the pencil line.

2 Glue the Cover

Fold over and glue the two flaps by the spine to the back of the paper. Using a flat-tipped paintbrush, brush glue onto the cover of the address book. Glue the address book to the bronze metallic paper rectangle. Smooth well to eliminate any air bubbles. Brush glue onto the paper flaps, fold and glue to the inside of the address book cover. Allow to dry under a weight.

3 Secure the Ribbon

Cut the ribbon in two. Incise a 3/16 in. (5 mm) vertical slit in the cover of the address book centered along height and 5/8 in. (1.5 cm) from the edge. Insert the end of one ribbon. Do the same in the back cover and insert the other ribbon. Thread a bead onto the ends of each ribbon and make a knot to secure it in place.

4 Gild the Initials

Cut out the chosen letters along with their backing. Using a paintbrush, brush on a coat of gilding size onto the initials and allow to dry. Adhere the gold leaf. Remove the letters from their backing and attach them to the address book cover.

5 Glue the End Papers

From the gold metallic paper, cut two 6 1/2x4 5/8 in. (16.3x11.8 cm) rectangles. Brush the glue onto the inside front and back covers, and onto the first and last pages of the address book. Glue on the end papers. Smooth and allow to dry under a weight.

SUGGESTION. *To make the initials, you can use gold-colored adhesive letters or paint them with gold acrylic paint.*

Applying the Gold Leaf

Before all else, you need to brush the gilding size onto the surface you wish to gild (this special glue becomes sticky once it dries). The gold leaf should be positioned and smoothed very gently with a dry paintbrush. Gold leaves are extremely thin and delicate: in case of tears, overlap the pieces on the surface to be gilded and smooth with a dry paintbrush.

A Rétro Note Pad

Tools

- Ruler
- Utility knife
- Cutting mat
- Scissors
- Compass with adaptor
- Rotary cutter
- Fine-tipped paintbrush
- Hole punch (9/32 in. [7 mm] in diameter)

Materials

- 4 1/4x6 in. (11x15 cm) spiral pad
- 3 1/8x3 1/8 in. (8x8 cm) acetate square
- 5 1/2x7 1/4 in. (14x18.5 cm) sheet of 1/32 in. (1 mm) thick chipboard
- Two A3 sheets of black faux leather paper
- Two 4 1/8x6 in. (10.5x15 cm) rectangles (A) of 3/16 in. (5 mm) thick foam board
- One 1 1/2x4 3/4 in. (4x12 cm) rectangle (B) of 1/8 in. (3 mm) thick foam board
- 4x6 in. (10x15 cm) sheet of white paper
- Fine point black permanent marker
- Ten white stickers, 5/16 in. (8 mm) in diameter
- Two silver holographic stickers
- 1/4 in. (6 mm) tall transferable numbers
- Adhesive letters
- 3/8 in. (1 cm) black double-sided adhesive foam circles
- 5 3/4 in. (40 cm) of black electrical cable
- Adhesive tape
- Elmer's glue
- Universal fast-drying adhesive

Diff./Time

Difficult

1 hour and 30 min.

Here is an ideal cover for an address book: a retro telephone made of chipboard, foam board and black faux leather paper.

1 Create the Base

Photocopy the template. Transfer the diagram of the base onto the chipboard. Cut along solid lines. Score the folds by lightly passing over the dashed lines with a utility knife. Apply fast-drying adhesive to the flaps and glue the foam board rectangle A on top. Brush on Elmer's glue and cover with the black faux leather paper. Cover the second foam board rectangle A with the black faux leather paper in the same way.

2 Create the Receiver

Transfer the image of the receiver onto the foam board rectangle B and cut it out with a utility knife. Cover one side and the edge of the foam board with the black faux leather paper using Elmer's glue (to be able to fold the paper around the curves, cut into the edges of the paper with scissors and fold over the small flaps one after the other). Cover the back: transfer the image of the receiver to the back of the black faux leather paper, cut it out and glue it.

3 Create the Wheel

Cut a 2 1/2 in. (6.5 cm) circle from the white paper and from the acetate. Using the hole punch, make ten holes along the edge of the acetate circle. Stack the circles and trace the edges of the small circles onto the white circle with a black marker. Transfer the numbers, from 0 to 9, onto the white stickers and attach them to the paper circle. Attach the acetate to the paper with a black double-sided adhesive foam circle. Attach a holographic sticker to the center of the acetate. Using a marker, draw a line in the center of the sticker.

4 Compose the Title

From a piece of scrap white paper, cut a 5/8x5 3/4 in. (1.5x14.5 cm) strip. Round the corners with scissors. Using adhesive letters, compose the words "PHONE NUMBERS".

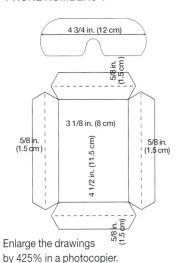

Enlarge the drawings by 425% in a photocopier.

5 Assemble the Components

Cut a 4 3/4x12 cm (12x30 cm) rectangle from black faux leather paper. Brush Elmer's glue on its back and fold in half obtaining a 4 3/4x6 in. (12x15 cm) rectangle. Glue it to the note pad to hide the spiral. Allow to dry. Using fast-drying adhesive, glue the foam board rectangle A to the back of the note pad and the base to the front. Attach the wheel, the receiver and the title with black double-sided adhesive foam pads.

Create the Details

Attach one end of the electrical cable below the receiver with adhesive tape. Fold the other end into the note pad's spiral. Cut a triangle from a holographic sticker and round the corners with scissors to create the finger stop; attach it to the wheel, to the right of number 9.

A Travel Address Book

Tools
- Pencil
- Ruler
- Utility knife
- Cutting mat
- Scissors
- Bone folder
- Flat-tipped paintbrush
- Paper clamps
- Riveting kit

Materials
- A3 red card stock
- Chipboard
- An old tourist guide
- Lined notebook
- Two metal rings
- 10 in. (25 cm) of blue or white ribbon
- Glue stick
- Elmer's glue

Diff./Time

Easy

1 hour and 30 min.

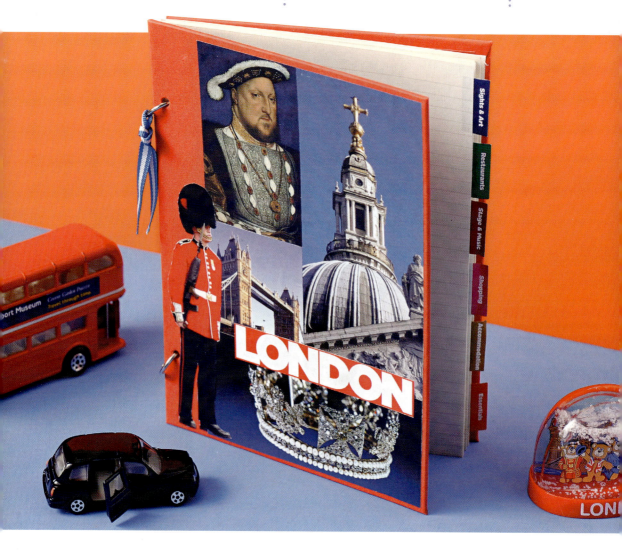

To remember your last trip, gather all the addresses in this address book with a cover full of photos of your destination.

1 Cut the Paper

Cut two 6x8 1/4 in. (15x21 cm) rectangles from chipboard and two 7x9 1/2 in. (18x24 cm) rectangles from red card stock. Cut six 6x8 1/4 in. (15x21 cm) rectangles from the notebook. Using scissors, cut photographs from the internal pages of the guide, which you will use to decorate the cover. Cut two 5 1/2x8 in. (14x20 cm) pages from the guide (playbills or advertisements) to decorate the inside covers.

2 Wrap the Covers

Brush Elmer's glue to one side of both chipboard rectangles. Glue one red card stock rectangle to the center of each. Using scissors, cut away the corners of the red card stock 1/32 in. (1 mm) from the chipboard.

3 Decorate the Cover

Arrange the photos cut out in step 1 on the cover like a mosaic (set them side to side leaving a 1 in (2.5 cm) border along the left edge and a 1/16 in. (2 mm) border along the other three edges). Cut out the subject of one of the photos with scissors. Cut out the name of the city. Attach the photos and the writing using the glue stick. Allow to dry under a weight for about 15 minutes.

IDEA. *You can increase the number of pages in the note pad but make sure to choose a suitable ring.*

Make the Finishing Touches

Score the red card stock flush with the chipboard rectangles using the bone folder. Brush Elmer's glue onto the card stock flaps and fold them over the edge of the chipboard. Attach the two advertisements to the insides of the covers using a glue stick. Place a weight on top of the two covers and allow to dry.

4 Make the Holes

On the illustrated cover, draw reference marks 1 1/2 in. (4 cm) from the upper and lower edges and 9/32 in. (7 mm) from the left edge. Using the hammer and the punch from the riveting kit, make holes in correspondance with the marks. Place this cover on top of the other and secure with paper clamps. Mark the location of the holes. Punch holes in the second cover. Mark the hole locations on the pages. Make holes in the pages.

5 Assemble

Place the back cover onto the working surface and set the pages and the illustrated cover on top. Insert the metal rings into the holes. Tie the ribbon to one of the rings. Cut words out of the travel guide to use as dividers. Attach these cutouts offset behind the pages with a glue stick.

All the photographs belong to Éditions Atlas except:
pages 1 top right, 2, 5 and 64, donatas1205/123RF;
page 1 bottom and 3 bottom, fojaga/123RF;
page 3 top, Andrei Kuzmik/123RF; page 3 bottom, fojaga/123RF;
cover: top left, donatas1205/123RF; back cover: top and center right,
donatas1205/123RF; bottom left, fojaga/123RF

© Éditions Atlas, Paris 2007

For the English edition:

WS White Star Publishers® is a registered trademark
belonging to De Agostini Libri S.p.A.

© 2016 De Agostini Libri S.p.A.
Via G. da Verrazano, 15
28100 Novara, Italy
www.whitestar.it - www.deagostini.it

Translation and Editing: TperTradurre S.R.L.

The rights to the total or partial translation,
reproduction or adaptation by any means are
reserved in all countries.

ISBN 978-88-544-0956-9
1 2 3 4 5 6   20 19 18 17 16

Printed in Italy

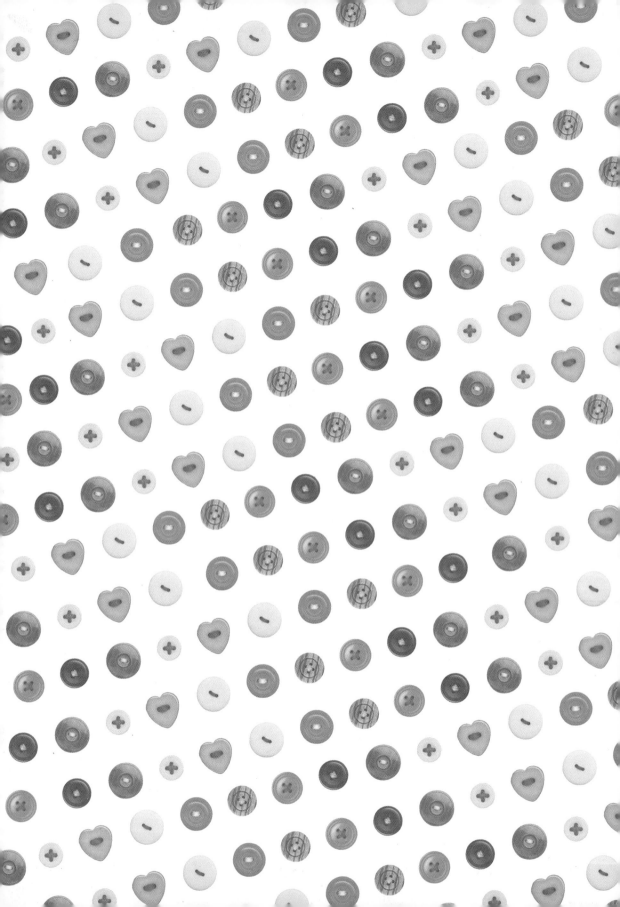